Hymns
FOR THE ANXIOUS HEART

ALEXA HESS

DISCLAIMER

Any diagnosis of clinical anxiety must come from a medical professional who is qualified to diagnose and treat such physiological symptoms. You should never attempt to self-diagnose. If you think you may be struggling with clinical anxiety, please seek the help of a qualified mental health professional. We hope that this study will be an encouragement to you regardless of the nature of your anxiety, as God and His Word speak to every condition, physical or spiritual. And we can cling to His Word even as we partake of the physical blessings of professional help and means of care that He provides to meet specific needs that we have.

HYMNS IN THIS RESOURCE

04	TURN YOUR EYES UPON JESUS
08	IT IS WELL
12	A MIGHTY FORTRESS IS OUR GOD
16	BE STILL, MY SOUL
20	HOW FIRM A FOUNDATION
24	WHAT A FRIEND WE HAVE IN JESUS
28	GREAT IS THY FAITHFULNESS
32	AMAZING GRACE
36	I NEED THEE EVERY HOUR
40	ROCK OF AGES
44	O GOD, OUR HELP IN AGES PAST
48	ABIDE WITH ME
52	HE WILL HOLD ME FAST
56	AFFLICTED SAINT, TO CHRIST DRAW NEAR
60	LEANING ON THE EVERLASTING ARMS
64	MY HOPE IS BUILT ON NOTHING LESS
68	BLESSED ASSURANCE
72	HIS EYE IS ON THE SPARROW
76	WONDERFUL PEACE
80	'TIS SO SWEET TO TRUST IN JESUS

Turn Your Eyes Upon Jesus

HELEN HOWARTH LEMMEL (1922)

O soul, are you weary and troubled?
No light in the darkness you see?
There's light for a look at the Savior,
And life more abundant and free!

CHORUS
Turn your eyes upon Jesus,
Look full in His wonderful face,
And the things of earth will grow strangely dim,
In the light of His glory and grace.

Thro' death into life everlasting,
He passed, and we follow Him there;
O'er us sin no more hath dominion—
For more than conqu'rors we are!

His Word shall not fail you—He promised;
Believe Him, and all will be well:
Then go to a world that is dying,
His perfect salvation to tell!

TURN YOUR EYES UPON JESUS

Where do you look when you are anxious? Do you become consumed with your own thoughts? Do you look to what is around you for comfort? Where we turn has a great influence on our minds. What we choose to focus on can shape our thoughts and provide a sense of anchoring in moments of fear. However, there are times when we do not know where to look. Anxiety can become so fierce that we feel hopeless and helpless, overwhelmed as we fixate on our fear.

Jesus desires for us to turn to Him when we are anxious. He wants us to refrain from fixating on the things around us or the thoughts in our minds as we look solely and fully at His face, trusting Him in our circumstances. When we look to Jesus, we are reminded of who He is. We are reminded that He is gentle and kind, that He extends to us grace and compassion. We are reminded that He is strong and powerful, that He is able to carry our burdens and fight our fears. And most of all, we are reminded that He is victorious, that He has won the battle over sin and death. These qualities of Jesus cause us to fixate on what is true amidst our fears. When we look to Jesus, we see more fully how the cares of the world are not as weighty as we first thought. We see more fully how our fears are not as powerful as we make them out to be. Our comfort in times of fear is that Jesus is bigger than our fears. But we can only rest in this truth by choosing to turn our eyes upon Him.

> *When we look to Jesus, we are reminded of who He is.*

In Matthew 14, there is a story of one of Jesus's disciples, Peter, walking on water with Jesus. As the story goes, when Peter walked toward Jesus on the water, his gaze faltered. His eyes were on Jesus, but they shifted to the wind blowing around him and the waves gushing at his feet. One moment, Peter was walking confidently, and the next moment, he was sinking. Peter's story reminds us of what we often do in moments of anxiety. We can sometimes tend to fixate upon our circumstances instead of the One who has control over our circumstances. As a result, we sink more deeply into the waters of anxiety. But Jesus wants us to fix our gaze on Him, for He is the only One who can keep us afloat. Looking to Jesus steadies us, reminding us how Jesus is the One helping us and strengthening us. It was Jesus's power that kept Peter from sinking, and it is His power that keeps us, too, from sinking into fear.

When we turn to Jesus in our anxiety, the things of this world will grow dim as the light of His presence becomes brighter than the darkness of our fears. We do not have to drown in our anxieties—all we must do is turn our eyes upon our Savior.

> *Jesus desires for us to turn to Him when we are anxious.*

PRAYER

Jesus, help me look to You when I am afraid. Keep me from focusing on my fear, and help me to focus on You instead. Remind me that You are bigger than the fears that seem big to me and greater than the circumstances that seem great to me. Remind me that You are there to help me when fear rises, and looking to You will keep me steady and calm. Thank You that You are always with me, that Your peace and strength are always carrying me. May I look fully to You in every moment of fear.

It is Well

HORATIO GATES SPAFFORD (1873)

When peace like a river attendeth my way,
when sorrows like sea billows roll;
whatever my lot, Thou hast taught me to say,
"It is well, it is well with my soul."

CHORUS
It is well with my soul;
it is well, it is well with my soul.
Though Satan should buffet, though trials should come,
let this blest assurance control:
that Christ has regarded my helpless estate,
and has shed His own blood for my soul.

My sin oh, the bliss of this glorious thought!
my sin, not in part, but the whole,
is nailed to the cross, and I bear it no more;
praise the Lord, praise the Lord, O my soul!

O Lord, haste the day when my faith shall be sight,
the clouds be rolled back as a scroll;
the trump shall resound and the Lord shall descend;
even so, it is well with my soul.

IT IS WELL

The circumstances of our lives can greatly disturb our souls. The anxiety we feel from life's troubles and trials can make us say, "It is not well with my soul." The anxious thoughts in our minds and the distress of our souls reveal to us the reality of suffering. When God created the world, creation was declared good. Now, the world we live in is deeply broken because of sin, and suffering inflicts every person. The hardships and sufferings of this life influence our anxiety and contribute to the fear that swells within us.

When Horatio G. Spafford wrote "It Is Well," his circumstances were certainly not good. Spafford's four daughters had just died in a shipwreck, and Spafford was on his way to meet his wife, who survived. It is believed that Spafford penned this hymn as he passed over the area of the sea where his daughters had died. It may be surprising to us that Spafford could write such a hymn of contentment in his time of deep suffering. Yet Spafford's words teach us how we can have contentment, even in anxiety, by trusting in the Lord. Spafford's sorrows may have billowed like the sea, but his soul trusted God.

> *When anxiety arises, we must not dwell on the circumstances that fuel our anxiety.*

The lyrics of "It Is Well" echo Paul's words in Philippians 4:11: "I have learned to be content in whatever circumstances I find myself." Throughout Paul's life, he experienced beating, stoning, imprisonment, starvation, and like Spafford, he was no stranger to shipwreck. Yet Paul's contentment did not lie in his circumstances but in his relationship with Christ. Like Spafford, even when life shifted and suffering arose, Paul clung to what remained: Jesus. Paul was able to withstand the hardships that came his way as he trusted in Jesus and rested in the strength Christ provided.

When anxiety arises, we must not dwell on the circumstances that fuel our anxiety. Instead, we must cling to the strength Christ gives us and trust Him. Christ remains, even when change comes or tragedy strikes. This promise of Christ's continual presence and power in our lives settles our anxious minds and calms our troubled souls.

It is the gospel that gives us utmost security when anxiety seeks to sway us. The good news of the gospel declares that because of Jesus's sacrifice, our sin has been defeated. We do not bear the weight of our sin and shame, for Christ has nailed our sin and shame to the cross. Ultimately, it is well with our souls because our souls have been rescued from the punishment of death. Our souls are secure in Christ's salvation, and no amount of anxiety can rip us from our salvation and eternal hope in Christ.

So whatever it may be that currently makes you anxious, do not allow it to take your eyes off what is true in Christ. Even when anxiety rises, your security in Christ allows you to say, "It is well with my soul."

Christ remains, even when change comes or tragedy strikes.

PRAYER

Dear Lord, thank You for the security found in You. Thank You that even when the circumstances of life make me overwhelmed and anxious, I can find comfort and contentment in You. Help me trust in You when suffering comes and anxiety strikes. Help me remember the truth of my salvation and the hope of my future with You. You have saved my soul; therefore, it is well with my soul.

A Mighty Fortress is our God

MARTIN LUTHER (1529)

A mighty fortress is our God,
a bulwark never failing;
our helper He, amid the flood
of mortal ills prevailing.
For still our ancient foe
does seek to work us woe;
his craft and power are great,
and armed with cruel hate,
on earth is not his equal.

Did we in our own strength confide,
our striving would be losing,
were not the right Man on our side,
the Man of God's own choosing.
You ask who that may be?
Christ Jesus, it is He;
Lord Sabaoth His name,
from age to age the same;
and He must win the battle.

And though this world, with devils filled,
should threaten to undo us,
we will not fear, for God has willed
His truth to triumph through us.
The prince of darkness grim,
we tremble not for him;
his rage we can endure,
for lo! his doom is sure;
one little word shall fell him.

That Word above all earthly powers
no thanks to them abideth;
the Spirit and the gifts are ours
through Him who with us sideth.
Let goods and kindred go,
this mortal life also;
the body they may kill:
God's truth abideth still;
His kingdom is forever!

A MIGHTY FORTRESS IS OUR GOD

When anxious thoughts arise, our anxiety can make us long for a sense of security. We are desperate to have something we can run to that makes us feel safe. Often, we run to other people or rely on our own strength for that security. But sadly, neither others nor ourselves can provide the lasting safety and security we desire.

This hymn by Martin Luther reminds us of David's words in Psalm 18:2: "The Lord is my rock, my fortress, and my deliverer, my God, my rock where I seek refuge, my shield and the horn of my salvation, my stronghold." As believers in Christ, we have a constant source of security. God is our mighty fortress to whom we can run in times of fear. As an all-powerful, never-changing God, He is like a fortress whose walls can never crumble. Nothing can break down our God—He is indestructible, the only stronghold we ever need.

> *The battle against anxiety has already been won.*

When we run to God in times of fear, we find security and protection in His powerful presence. As He holds us, He gives us His peace that guards our hearts and minds in Christ Jesus (Philippians 4:7). His peace soothes our worries and keeps anxious thoughts from overwhelming us. Without Christ, we would have nothing to protect us from anxious thoughts. Often, the enemy uses anxious thoughts to try and break down our faith. He tries to shoot arrows of condemnation and doubt in an attempt to make us feel hopeless and ashamed. But Christ is with us in the battle of anxiety and in the battle against the enemy. By His power, He thwarts the schemes of the enemy and gives us strength to fight the anxiety that seeks to overtake us.

Even if anxiety refuses to lift, we can find comfort, for Christ has already declared victory over sin and death. The battle against anxiety has already been won. One day, Christ will return and declare His final victory, removing sin and death forever. Because of this truth, the anxiety we feel is only temporary. And when that anxiety rises, may we lean into God's power to fight against our fears and hope in the victory that is to come.

God stands as our mighty fortress in the flood of fear. But we must come to Him. Let us run to Him and seek refuge there. Let us allow Him to fight for us when we feel too weak to fight. Let us rest in His peace that surpasses all understanding.

PRAYER

Thank You, God, that You are my Mighty Fortress. Forgive me for the times I run to other things or rely on myself to feel strong and secure. You are my only source of true strength and security. Lord, please guard my heart and mind against anxiety. Help me feel Your powerful and protective peace right now. Give me strength to fight this battle, and help me hope in the final victory that is to come.

Be Still, My Soul

KATHARINA VON SCHLEGEL
TRANSLATOR: JANE BORTHWICK (1855)

Be still, my soul! For God is on your side;
bear patiently the cross of grief or pain:
leave to your God to order and provide,
who through all changes faithful will remain.
Be still, my soul! Your best, your heav'nly Friend
through thorny ways leads to a joyful end.

Be still, my soul! For God will undertake
to guide the future surely as the past.
Your hope, your confidence, let nothing shake;
all now mysterious shall be clear at last.
Be still, my soul! The waves and winds still know
the voice that calmed their fury long ago.

Be still, my soul! The hour is hastening on
when we shall be forever in God's peace;
when disappointment, grief, and fear are gone,
love's joys restored, our strivings all shall cease.
Be still, my soul! When change and tears are past,
all safe and blessed we shall meet at last.

BE STILL, MY SOUL

Anxiety can often make us feel like a ship on a storm-tossed sea, with each wave of anxiety hitting us and throwing us off course. We can read the words of this hymn and wonder how to be still when our worry tosses us to and fro. But through this hymn, Katharina von Schlegel gives us four reasons why we can be still, even amid anxiety.

First, we can be still because God is on our side. Exodus 14:14 says, "The Lord will fight for you; you need only to be still" (NIV). In this verse, the Israelites were afraid they would be captured by Pharaoh's army. But Moses reminded them that it was God who fought for them, so they could simply be still. God is the One who gives us His strength and the promise that He is fighting with us and for us. We can be still, even in anxiety, knowing that God never leaves our side.

Second, we can be still because God holds our future. Often, the source of our worries is a fear of the future and the unknown. We can look to what is ahead or worry about what is to come with much anxiety. But instead of looking ahead in fear, we need to look to God in trust. In Psalm 46:10, God declares, "Be still, and know that I am God" (ESV). In moments of fear, we can rest in who God is. Our God is a sovereign God, who orchestrates all things for our good and His glory. Our God is a God of faithfulness, who never fails to keep His promises and will always come through for us, even if things seem uncertain. Our future is held in the hands of a faithful God, so we can trust Him with the unknown.

> *In moments of fear, we can rest in who God is.*

We can also be still because God is in control. When the disciples faced a fierce storm in Mark 4:39, Jesus stood up, rebuked the wind, and said, "Peace! Be still!" (ESV). The storm the disciples experienced may have been strong, but Jesus holds more power than any storm. Jesus has power over all of creation. Therefore, what seems out of control to us is held together in Christ's hands. In moments of anxiety, Jesus does not rebuke us like He did the waves, but He lovingly and kindly calls us to be still. He calls us to lay down what is causing us to fear and rest in the peace that He provides.

Lastly, we can be still because this life is only temporary. The things that are making us anxious will not last forever. As we press on through fear, we move toward an eternity where all fear will be gone, and all we will know is God's perfect peace. Though the storm of anxiety rages, our souls can be still as we rest in God's presence and promises.

> Jesus has power over all of creation.

PRAYER

Lord, thank You for who You are. Thank You for always being with me, for Your great faithfulness, and for Your peace. Help me trust in You when I feel afraid. Remind me of who You are when the future feels daunting, and remind me that I can trust You with the unknown. When anxiety arises, help my soul be still. Keep me from feeling shaken, and help me rest in Your peace.

How Firm a Foundation

K.; ATTRIBUTED TO GEORGE KEITH AND R. KEEN (C. 1787)

How firm a foundation, you saints of the Lord,
is laid for your faith in His excellent Word!
What more can He say than to you He has said,
to you who for refuge to Jesus have fled?

"Fear not, I am with you; O be not dismayed,
for I am your God, and will still give you aid.
I'll strengthen you, help you, and cause you to stand,
upheld by my righteous, omnipotent hand.

"When through the deep waters I call you to go,
the rivers of sorrow shall not overflow,
for I will be with you, your troubles to bless,
and sanctify to you the deepest distress.

"When through fiery trials your pathway shall lie,
My grace, all sufficient, shall be your supply.
The flames shall not hurt you. I only design
your dross to consume, and your gold to refine.

"The soul that on Jesus still leans for repose,
I will not, I will not desert to its foes.
That soul, though all hell should endeavor to shake,
I'll never, no never, no never forsake!"

HOW FIRM A FOUNDATION

Fear shakes the ground beneath our feet. We can feel perfectly fine and steady until something happens that awakens anxiety, and suddenly we are shaken. There would be no sense of stability in these moments without God's Word. God's Word keeps us stable because it reminds us what is true. Scripture declares that God's promises to us remain unshaken, even when the world itself seems to shake. In times of fear, God's Word is a firm foundation upon which we can rest.

Often, we feel unstable because we are not going to God's Word. Without the continual reminder of what God says to us through His Word, we have no truth to cling to in moments of anxiety. Distancing ourselves from God's Word only multiplies our anxiety. We need to run to Scripture and remain in Scripture so that we can speak its truth over ourselves. Through reading God's Word, we are reminded of treasured truths and promises that remain for God's people.

> *God's Word is a firm foundation upon which we can rest.*

Isaiah 41:10 is quoted in "How Firm a Foundation" to remind us of God's continual presence. Our fears can be quieted by knowing that God is with us, always helping and strengthening us. We can feel steady because God holds us with His mighty hand. Isaiah 43:2 is also quoted as a reminder that God's presence goes with us through fiery trials and troublesome floods. God is with us in both the good and bad times. When the floodwaters of fear rise, God is with us in those waters, keeping us from drowning under the weight of our fears. And when we have no choice but to walk through difficult trials, we do not walk alone. God walks with us in those times of trial, sanctifying us and giving us His strength to endure.

Lastly, Deuteronomy 31:8 is quoted to remind us that God never leaves us. Before Jesus ascended into heaven, He assured His disciples that He would be with them always (Matthew 28:20). As followers of Christ, God promises us that His presence will always be with us—we have been given the Holy Spirit who comes to dwell in us when we accept the Lord as our Savior. As believers, nothing can take away His presence from us, even when we struggle with sin or experience suffering.

All of the promises quoted in this hymn are drawn straight from Scripture, further solidifying the truth that God's Word is our firm foundation. We need these promises to keep us steady when life feels heavy and fears arise within us. God has graciously given us His Word, but we must regularly take up His Word and wield its truth against our anxious thoughts.

> *God is with us in both the good and bad times.*

PRAYER

Dear Lord, thank You for Your Word. Thank You for what You say to me through Your Word and for the promises You have spoken. Holy Spirit, please bring to mind the truth of God's Word when I am afraid. Remind me what is true and promised to me in Christ. Help me depend on God's Word and ground myself in Scripture's firm foundation. Whenever I feel shaken, steady me as I meditate on Your Word.

What a Friend We Have in Jesus

JOSEPH MEDLICOTT SCRIVEN (1855)

What a friend we have in Jesus,
all our sins and griefs to bear!
What a privilege to carry
everything to God in prayer!
O what peace we often forfeit,
O what needless pain we bear,
all because we do not carry
everything to God in prayer!

Have we trials and temptations?
Is there trouble anywhere?
We should never be discouraged;
take it to the Lord in prayer!
Can we find a friend so faithful
who will all our sorrows share?
Jesus knows our every weakness;
take it to the Lord in prayer!

Are we weak and heavy laden,
cumbered with a load of care?
Precious Savior, still our refuge —
take it to the Lord in prayer!
Do your friends despise, forsake you?
Take it to the Lord in prayer!
In His arms He'll take and shield you;
you will find a solace there.

WHAT A FRIEND WE HAVE IN JESUS

How often do we feel all alone when we are anxious? Anxiety can feel lonely because it often feels like people do not understand what we are experiencing. The enemy presses into these feelings of loneliness with his lies, seeking to isolate us. However, one of the sweetest realities of being a believer is that we are never alone. Even when we do feel alone, Christ remains our steadfast companion and faithful friend. He is always near to us and welcomes us to come to Him in prayer when we feel anxious and afraid.

Jesus is our greatest friend in times of fear because He knows exactly what we are going through. The enemy may whisper to us that no one truly understands, but Christ does. Before going to the cross, Jesus felt the burden of anxiety. He felt the weight of what He was about to do, and that weight was painful and agonizing. But then Jesus went on to experience intense suffering for our sake, willingly dying on the cross to bear our sin and shame. Jesus is no stranger to suffering. He understands what it is like to be afflicted and anxious. We are in an intimate relationship with One who knows our every weakness and perfectly sympathizes with us (Hebrews 4:15).

> *The enemy may whisper to us that no one truly understands, but Christ does.*

The fact that Jesus knows our pain and wants to help us in our pain should encourage us to come to Him. Hebrews 4:16 tells us that because Jesus sympathizes with our weakness that we can approach the throne of grace with boldness to receive mercy and find grace to help us in our every need. We can approach Jesus in prayer with absolute confidence, knowing that He welcomes us with unending grace and love.

Prayer is a powerful weapon against anxiety, yet often, we do not take advantage of the valuable gift it is. Instead of coming to Jesus, we often try to rely on our own strength to fight anxiety. When we choose to refrain from prayer, we forfeit the peace offered to us, forcing ourselves to bear the weight of our anxiety. But we do not have to remain this way. Jesus stands by our side, ready and willing to help us combat our anxious thoughts. He desires to carry our burdens and provide us with His peace when we come to Him.

We can take everything that we are feeling and experiencing to Jesus. His arms are forever open wide to us, lovingly welcoming us to seek solace in His embrace. May we see our moments of anxiety as opportunities to pray. Instead of dwelling on anxious thoughts, let us direct our thoughts to Jesus in prayer. May we take all of our anxiety to Jesus, asking for His help and resting in the peace He provides. We are never alone in our moments of anxiety. Jesus is our steadfast friend who never leaves our side.

> *We are never alone in our moments of anxiety. Jesus is our steadfast friend who never leaves our side.*

PRAYER

Jesus, thank You for being my faithful friend. Thank You that You are always near to me and always available for me to come to You in prayer. Forgive me for the times I refuse to come to You and try to depend on my own strength. Help me continually see my need for You, especially in moments of anxiety. May I take all that I am feeling to You in prayer so that You can carry my burdens and fill me with Your peace that passes all understanding.

Great is Thy Faithfulness

THOMAS O. CHISHOLM (1923)

Great is Thy faithfulness, O God my Father.
There is no shadow of turning with Thee.
Thou changest not, Thy compassions, they fail not.
As Thou hast been Thou forever wilt be.

CHORUS

Great is Thy faithfulness!
Great is Thy faithfulness!
Morning by morning new mercies I see.
All I have needed Thy hand hath provided.
Great is Thy faithfulness, Lord, unto me!

Summer and winter, and springtime and harvest,
sun, moon, and stars in their courses above,
join with all nature in manifold witness
to Thy great faithfulness, mercy, and love.

Pardon for sin and a peace that endureth,
Thine own dear presence to cheer and to guide,
strength for today and bright hope for tomorrow;
blessings all mine, with ten thousand beside!

GREAT IS THY FAITHFULNESS

God is a God of faithfulness. It is in His nature to fulfill what He has promised and to follow through with what He says. However, when we worry, we can often forget this attribute of God. Our anxiety can take our eyes off of God's faithfulness, causing us to worry about the things we need. We too easily forget how God has been faithful to us in the past as we worry about what is happening in the present and what will happen in the future. We need the continual reminder of God's faithfulness to set our hearts and minds on what is true: God always has and always will take care of us.

When Jesus encouraged His followers not to be anxious in Matthew 6:25-34, He reminded them of God's faithfulness. Jesus drew attention to the birds of the sky and the wildflowers of the field to demonstrate God's great care for His creation and His greater care for us. Jesus tells us that God knows and will provide all we need. Therefore, we do not need to worry about where our provision will come from—we need only to trust the Provider. All we have needed, God's gracious hand has provided. He has always been faithful to us. We belong to a heavenly Father who takes care of His children, who provides His children with exactly what they need.

God is a God of faithfulness.

But God has also demonstrated His faithfulness by providing what we need for everlasting life. God could have left us without a way for salvation, but He did not. From the beginning, He put forth a plan to bring His people forgiveness and salvation, and by His faithfulness, He fulfilled that plan through Jesus Christ. Because God has been faithful to provide our greatest spiritual need, He will surely be faithful to provide our physical needs as well.

The forgiveness we have received through Christ causes us to proclaim, "Great is Thy faithfulness!" But we can also proclaim God's great faithfulness in every area of our lives. When we feel anxious, we must remember who God is and what He has done for us. We must look back and remind ourselves of the ways God has worked to sovereignly provide and bless us. We must look around and remind ourselves of what God has currently given to us—that the shoes on our feet and the food in our stomachs are because of His grace. And with those reminders, we look with confidence to the future, trusting that God will be faithful still.

Every day, we can be reminded of God's continual blessings—that His mercy is new every morning and that He blesses us with daily strength and eternal hope. Even when materials run out, God's mercy and grace will continue. His compassion will never shift, even when our circumstances change. We can trust Him with our every worry. Faithful He has been, and faithful He will always be.

> *Even when materials run out, God's mercy and grace will continue.*

PRAYER

God, thank You that Your mercies are new every morning. Thank You for being a good Father, who cares for His children and provides for them. Forgive me for the times I fail to trust Your faithfulness or forget Your faithfulness. You have always been good to me, and You will always be good to me. When I am anxious, help me trust that You are taking care of me. Help me trust that You will continue to be faithful, even if I cannot see what You are doing or how You will provide. Great is Your faithfulness to me.

Amazing Grace

JOHN NEWTON (1779)

Amazing grace (how sweet the sound)
that saved a wretch like me!
I once was lost, but now am found,
was blind, but now I see.

'Twas grace that taught my heart to fear,
and grace my fears relieved;
how precious did that grace appear
the hour I first believed!

Through many dangers, toils and snares
I have already come:
'tis grace has brought me safe thus far,
and grace will lead me home.

The Lord has promised good to me,
His Word my hope secures;
He will my shield and portion be
as long as life endures.

Yes, when this flesh and heart shall fail,
and mortal life shall cease:
I shall possess, within the veil,
a life of joy and peace.

The earth shall soon dissolve like snow,
the sun forbear to shine;
but God, who called me here below,
will be forever mine.

AMAZING GRACE

We may have heard the hymn "Amazing Grace" many times without contemplating its significance. What made God's grace truly amazing for the hymn's author, John Newton, was his personal testimony. Newton spent many years of his life as a slave trader. It was not until he became violently ill while at sea that he turned to God and abandoned his career. Newton's story reminds us of the story of the Apostle Paul, who encountered Jesus and was changed from a persecutor of Christians to a preacher of the gospel (Acts 9:1-30). Like Paul, Newton experienced a tremendous transformation, becoming an Anglican priest and using his ministry to fight slavery. Both Newton and Paul's testimonies speak to how God's grace given to us through Christ is a grace extended to anyone, no matter their history or mistakes.

> *We need Christ's grace every day of our lives.*

The grace that we receive in salvation is not a one-time transaction. We need Christ's grace every day of our lives. In fact, the Christian life hinges upon the grace of Christ. We are not only saved by Christ's grace but sustained by it. Because of Christ, we receive daily forgiveness and mercy for our sin, and we receive grace and strength for our weaknesses and shortcomings. It is because of Christ's grace that we can endure suffering and fight anxiety. All we have and will continue to have is due to the grace of God. We do not deserve Christ's grace, and we do nothing to earn Christ's grace. Christ's grace is a gift, and that is why it is so amazing.

Yet how often do we think about Christ's grace when we are anxious? Instead of resting in Christ's grace, we worry that God is upset with us for our anxiety. Maybe we see God as an unhappy father, with a frown on His face and crossed arms, berating us for being anxious instead of trusting Him. But that is not the Father we have, for God understands our suffering, and His grace is sufficient in our weakness (2 Corinthians 12:9). He stands with His loving arms open to us, ready to pour out His grace over us.

Christ's grace is good news for the anxious because His grace relieves our fears. Because Jesus has rescued us from the punishment of our sin, we no longer have to fear death. And not only this, but we do not have to fear anything we might face because God offers us His protection, strength, and peace. Even when we walk through trials and troubles, it is by God's grace that we are led through them. Even if fear paralyzes us and we feel as though we cannot take a step, God's grace will carry us forward. God's grace will lead us each day, through whatever life may bring, carrying us safely home into eternity with Him.

> *We are not only saved by Christ's grace but sustained by it.*

PRAYER

Jesus, thank You for Your grace. Thank You for saving me and daily sustaining me by Your grace. Help me to remember and rest in Your grace when I feel ashamed of my anxiety. Remind me that You love me and that Your grace flows over me, even when I am anxious. May I lean on Your grace when I feel worried, allowing Your grace to silence my fears. By Your amazing grace, You will take care of me and sustain me now and for all eternity to come.

I Need Thee Every Hour

ROBERT LOWRY; ANNIE S. HAWKS (1872)

I need Thee ev'ry hour,
Most gracious Lord;
No tender voice like Thine
Can peace afford.

CHORUS
I need Thee, oh, I need Thee;
Ev'ry hour I need Thee;
Oh, bless me now, my Savior,
I come to Thee.

I need Thee ev'ry hour,
Stay Thou nearby;
Temptations lose their pow'r
When Thou art nigh.

I need Thee ev'ry hour,
In joy or pain;
Come quickly and abide,
Or life is vain.

I need Thee ev'ry hour,
Teach me Thy will;
And Thy rich promises
In me fulfill.

I NEED THEE EVERY HOUR

As humans, how easy it is for us to think we are independent people. We like to think we have enough power, knowledge, and ability to do things on our own. And while we can do some things on our own, we soon realize that we cannot do everything on our own. Eventually, we find that we do not have enough strength, and we end up tiring and losing our energy. We find that we cannot do everything perfectly, that we make mistakes and have weaknesses. In these moments, we realize just how dependent we truly are.

Nothing shows us our need for dependency like anxiety. We may try with all of our might to handle anxiety on our own, but soon, we crumble under the weight of our worried minds. We find there is no way we can combat every anxious thought or have enough ability in ourselves to obtain calm and peace. However, instead of this reality moving us to despair, it should move us to hope in Jesus. In John 15:5, Jesus says that without Him, we can do nothing. As we go about our days, we do not flourish in our own strength but in Christ's. Because Jesus is the One who empowers us, He is the One we are to rely on in every moment.

> *He is the One we are to rely on in every moment.*

We need Jesus to give us the strength to fight against our anxious thoughts. We need His peace to help calm our fears and still our hearts. There is not one part of our day, one moment of anxiety, in which we do not need Jesus. In John 15, Jesus compares believers to branches and Himself to a vine. Jesus uses this imagery to illustrate our dependence on Him because branches are utterly dependent on the vine for stability and sustenance. Without the vine, the branches have no life. They need the vine in order to survive and thrive. In the same way, we need Jesus in order to have life. Only Jesus can give us salvation from our sin, granting us everlasting life. Only Jesus can offer us spiritual life by daily giving us His grace, strength, and peace.

Instead of trying to handle anxiety on our own, we must continually remember our need for Christ. We may feel ashamed to come to Him for help, but He welcomes us, eager to give us the help and strength we need. Our moments of insufficiency are opportunities to rest in Christ's sufficiency. We need Jesus in our battle with anxiety, so may we come to Him in full reliance and dependence for the strength and peace only He can provide.

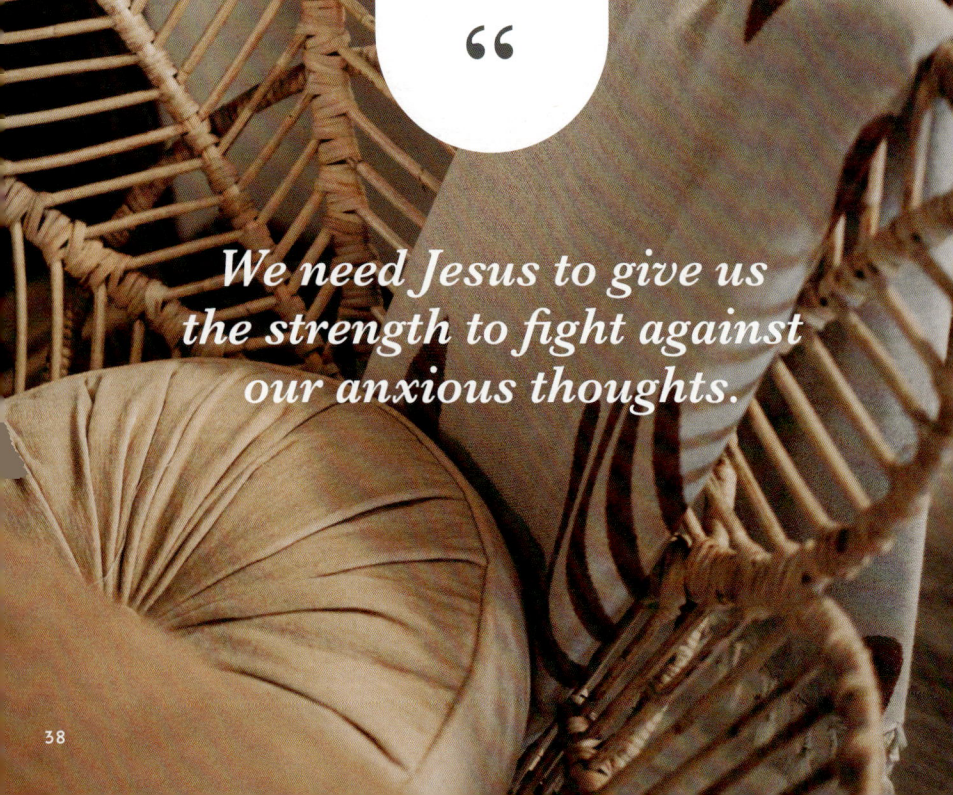

> We need Jesus to give us the strength to fight against our anxious thoughts.

PRAYER

Lord, forgive me for the times I disregard my need for You. Forgive me for trying to rely on my own strength and power instead of depending on You. Thank You that I have a constant source of strength, peace, and life through Your Son, Jesus. Thank You that I am never left defenseless or helpless, and all that I need is found in You. Help me rely on You when I am anxious and depend on You alone to give me peace. May I recognize my need for You in every struggle with fear, always turning to You for help.

Rock of Ages

AUGUSTUS TOPLADY (1776)

Rock of Ages, cleft for me,
let me hide myself in Thee;
let the water and the blood,
from Thy wounded side which flowed,
be of sin the double cure;
save from wrath and make me pure.

Not the labors of my hands
can fulfill Thy law's demands;
could my zeal no respite know,
could my tears forever flow,
all for sin could not atone;
Thou must save, and Thou alone.

Nothing in my hand I bring,
simply to the cross I cling;
naked, come to thee for dress;
helpless, look to thee for grace;
foul, I to the fountain fly;
wash me, Savior, or I die.

While I draw this fleeting breath,
when mine eyes shall close in death,
when I soar to worlds unknown,
see Thee on Thy judgment throne,
Rock of Ages, cleft for me,
let me hide myself in Thee.

ROCK OF AGES

Our worries and fears can make us feel unstable. We find ourselves searching for something strong and steadfast for security and are soon disappointed when we realize this world cannot offer the security and stability we so desire. However, it is that lack of stability that is meant to lead us to the Lord. God is our Rock, the only One who can give us a firm foundation—one that is forever steadfast and secure.

Throughout Scripture, God is often referred to as a rock. The psalmist says in Psalm 71:3, "Be a rock of refuge for me, where I can always go... you are my rock and fortress." The prophet Isaiah writes in Isaiah 26:4, "Trust in the Lord forever, because in the Lord, the Lord himself, is an everlasting rock!" A rock is large and not easily moved, and its weight and structure make it hard to break. Scripture uses the imagery of God as a rock because God is strong and mighty, all-powerful and indestructible. Nothing can move Him.

He will cover and protect us.

While God is holy and mighty, He is also kind and compassionate. He is the perfect Rock to run to because His power keeps us safe, and His kindness welcomes us to find safety in Him. In Exodus 33:21-23, God would not allow Moses to see His face, for the reality of His glory would be deadly. Instead, He promised to show Moses His back after He passed by him. He told Moses, "Here is a place near me. You are to stand on the rock, and when my glory passes by, I will put you in the crevice of the rock and cover you with my hand until I have passed by." This story of God placing Moses in a rock for protection is a picture of what God does for us. In times of fear, God brings us into His presence and gives us a place to hide within Himself.

But we would not be able to experience the safety God provides without Jesus. Jesus is our Rock of Ages, broken on the cross for our sake. Christ's sacrifice on the cross reconciles us with God, making it possible for us to have a relationship with a holy and mighty God without fear of wrath or punishment. Our relationship with God, given to us through Christ, allows God to be a permanent place of refuge for us.

Anxiety can make us feel unsafe, but we are safe in God's hands. When anxiety causes us to desire safety, all we must do is come before the Lord. He will cover and protect us. He will be an indestructible cover for us as we rest and depend on Him. He can never be moved, and when we seek shelter in Him, neither will we be moved.

Anxiety can make us feel unsafe, but we are safe in God's hands.

PRAYER

Lord, thank You for being my everlasting Rock. Thank You that because of Your Son, my Rock of Ages, You are a constant source of safety and security for me. When anxiety rises, help me come to You to find rest. Keep me from looking to other things to provide the safety only You can provide. May Your powerful presence calm my mind and soothe my worries. Even if my outward circumstances cause me to fear, I know I am safe in You.

O God, Our Help in Ages Past

ISAAC WATTS (1719)

O God, our help in ages past,
our hope for years to come,
our shelter from the stormy blast,
and our eternal home;

under the shadow of Your throne
Your saints have dwelt secure.
Sufficient is Your arm alone,
and our defense is sure.

Before the hills in order stood,
or earth received its frame,
from everlasting You are God,
to endless years the same.

A thousand ages in Your sight
are like an evening gone,
short as the watch that ends the night
before the rising sun.

Time, like an ever-rolling stream,
soon bears us all away.
We fly forgotten, as a dream
dies at the op'ning day.

O God, our help in ages past,
our hope for years to come,
still be our guard while troubles last,
and our eternal home.

O GOD, OUR HELP IN AGES PAST

Our God is a God who cares for His people. Throughout Scripture—from the beginning to the end—we continually see how God has helped His people. Even when they rebelled against Him and were unfaithful, God was always faithful to provide for and take care of them. Yet why do we forget these truths in times of anxiety? We can read how God has helped His people for ages past but doubt that He will help us in the present. Though God has demonstrated His faithfulness to us over and over again, we worry that this time, He will not come through. But God's unchanging character attests to the truth that He will always help us, take care of us, and provide for us—now and forever.

Psalm 121:1-2 says, "I lift my eyes toward the mountains. Where will my help come from? My help comes from the Lord, the Maker of heaven and earth." When God's help is declared in the psalms, it is usually in a time of trouble, fear, or danger. In this instance, the psalmist knew that there was no one else who could help him fight his enemies or save him from disaster. Only God could provide him with exactly what he needed. God is our greatest help in our greatest need.

God is always ready to help us in our battle with anxiety.

But why do we not always first come to Him for help when we are afraid? Why do we doubt that He will take care of us when we are anxious? There is little we can do in our own strength to help us in times of anxiety—we need the help of the Lord. We must come to Him. We must receive the help He offers us: His peace for our fears, His strength for our weaknesses, and His comfort for our afflictions. God is always ready to help us in our battle with anxiety. We simply need to come to Him and receive the help He provides.

One of the best ways to be reminded of God's continual help is by going to Scripture. When we open the pages of Scripture, we can read of how God came to the aid of the Israelites when they were enslaved in Egypt. We can read of how God provided food for the Israelites in the wilderness and kept them safe as they traveled to the Promised Land. We can read of how God helped defeat the Israelites' enemies and restored them after their exile. And most importantly, we can read of how God provided us with the solution for our greatest need by giving us salvation through Christ. Not once did God relinquish His care for His people then, and neither will He relinquish His care for us today.

Because God is our helper, we can trust Him. We can always trust Him to be our shelter in times of fear and our defense against our anxious thoughts. He is our help in ages past, and He will be our help for ages still to come.

Because God is our helper, we can trust Him.

PRAYER

Lord, thank You for being my helper. Thank You that You are a God who promises to remain a constant aid for His people. When I am anxious, remind me that You are my helper. Remind me of the many times You have helped me in the past, and remind me that You will always continue to help me. In times of fear, help me to move toward You through prayer and Your Word. Keep me from trying to rely on myself, and encourage me to go to You for help instead.

Abide With Me
HENRY FRANCIS LYTE (1847)

Abide with me: fast falls the eventide;
the darkness deepens; Lord, with me abide.
When other helpers fail and comforts flee,
Help of the helpless, O abide with me.

Swift to its close ebbs out life's little day;
earth's joys grow dim, its glories pass away.
Change and decay in all around I see.
O Thou who changest not, abide with me.

I need Thy presence every passing hour.
What but Thy grace can foil the tempter's power?
Who like Thyself my guide and strength can be?
Through cloud and sunshine, O abide with me.

I fear no foe with Thee at hand to bless,
ills have no weight, and tears no bitterness.
Where is death's sting? Where, grave, thy victory?
I triumph still, if Thou abide with me.

Hold Thou Thy cross before my closing eyes.
Shine through the gloom and point me to the skies.
Heaven's morning breaks and earth's vain shadows flee;
in life, in death, O Lord, abide with me.

ABIDE WITH ME

For many of us, there is something so comforting about being home. A home should be safe and a place where we can rest. When we are anxious, it can be hard for many of us to leave our homes because we do not want to venture from the comfort and security we find there. But as believers, we have a permanent home in Christ. Even when we step out of our homes, we have a permanent place of comfort and rest in Jesus. Henry Francis Lyte drew inspiration for this hymn from John 15, in which Jesus calls us to abide in Him. To abide in Christ is similar to being in the comfort of a home. In Christ, we are given a safe place to abide—a place to live, rest, and remain.

Jesus says in John 14:23, "If anyone loves me, he will keep my word. My Father will love him, and we will come to him and make our home with him." Jesus describes how those who trust and believe in Him have the presence of God dwelling within them. When we come to know Christ, the Holy Spirit comes to make His home inside of us. Therefore, we are never without the presence of the Lord. He abides with us forever.

He abides with us forever.

The fact that Jesus abides with us means we can never be separated from Him. We belong to Him, and Him to us, in a union that can never be broken. Our anxious thoughts can never tear Him away or scare Him away. Even when anxiety makes us feel that Christ is not near, He is always near to us. When our circumstances shift and change, Jesus remains constant. When all other comforts and helpers fail, Jesus is our comforter and helper who remains. Because Jesus is the helper of the helpless, He is our strength when we feel helpless in our fight against anxiety.

Christ's presence with us also reminds us of the future that is to come. Jesus abides with us now through His Holy Spirit, and we have the promise of an eternity of peace with Him. Jesus has already declared victory over sin and suffering, and one day, we will see Him declare victory once and for all when He returns. Even though anxiety can so often make us feel weak, we have victory over our anxiety because of Christ. We can triumph in moments of fear, for we know anxiety will not have the final word.

Yet, we can lose sight of these treasured truths when we are afraid. Our anxiety can make it hard for us to feel Christ's presence, peace, and provision. In these moments, we can follow the words of this hymn by praying, "Jesus, abide with me." We can ask Jesus to make His presence known to us, to help us feel His power and peace. The peace and strength of Christ encourage us to continually remain in His presence. Jesus is our home of refuge in times of fear, so may we abide with Him as He abides with us.

> *When our circumstances shift and change, Jesus remains constant.*

PRAYER

Jesus, thank You for the union we share because of Your mercy and grace. Thank You that I belong to You and that You abide with me always. Help me remember that You abide with me when I am anxious — that in You, I am secure and sustained. Help me remain close to You as You remain close to me. When I feel alone, remind me that You are with me and that Your presence gives me peace and strength. May I abide with You, Jesus, and rejoice that You forever abide with me.

He Will Hold Me Fast

ADA R. HABERSHON (1906)

When I fear my faith will fail,
Christ will hold me fast;
When the tempter would prevail,
He can hold me fast!

CHORUS
He will hold me fast,
He will hold me fast;
For my Savior loves me so,
He will hold me fast.

I could never keep my hold,
He must hold me fast;
For my love is often cold,
He must hold me fast.

I am precious in His sight,
He will hold me fast;
Those He saves are His delight,
He will hold me fast.

He'll not let my soul be lost,
Christ will hold me fast;
Bought by Him at such a cost,
He will hold me fast.

HE WILL HOLD ME FAST

What incredible comfort for children when they are held in the arms of someone who loves them. Often when a child has a nightmare or is hurt, being swept up in an embrace by a caring adult or loved one brings instant relief. As adults, we still find comfort in an embrace from those who love us. However, it can be hard to find this kind of comfort when we are anxious, especially when no one is near. We long for someone to wrap their arms around us and tell us that everything is going to be okay.

As followers of Christ, we are promised this comfort, and Scripture tells us that Jesus never lets us go. In John 10:28-29, Jesus says of believers, "I give them eternal life, and they will never perish. No one will snatch them out of my hand. My Father, who has given them to me, is greater than all. No one is able to snatch them out of the Father's hand." The salvation we have received in Christ means that we are secure in Christ's grip, even when we struggle with sin or falter in our faith.

Christ's hold on us is more powerful than anxiety's hold on us. No matter how tumultuous anxiety may be, Jesus's steadfast hold remains through each of life's anxieties. Anxious thoughts may rain down, and fears may toss us to and fro, but Christ will remain our secure anchor. As we struggle to cling to Him, He faithfully clings to us.

> *As we struggle to cling to Him, He faithfully clings to us.*

Christ's hold on us encourages our hold on Him. In moments of anxiety, we can cling to Him tightly and rest in His embrace. Jesus is the person we are to rely on most when we are afraid, for only He can provide us with the sustaining security and comfort we so desire. In the moments when we are too weary to fight our anxiety, we can collapse into Christ's arms, where we can find peace in knowing that His steady hold will sustain us and carry us through. And not only this, but Christ promises to carry us to eternity. Because we can never leave His hands, our eternity with Him remains intact. Though anxiety may weigh heavily upon us in the present, we can cast those cares upon Him and rejoice that by His grace, He is carrying us to a future where anxiety will be no more.

When the world feels heavy, He will hold you fast. When your fears cloud your faith, He will hold you fast. When bad news comes, He will hold you fast. When your worst fears are realized, He will hold you fast. When lies are louder than God's truth, He will hold you fast. For now and forever, He will hold you fast.

> *When the world feels heavy, He will hold you fast. When your fears cloud your faith, He will hold you fast.*

PRAYER

Jesus, thank You that You are always holding onto me. Thank You that there is nothing I can do and nothing that can be done to me that will pull me from Your hands. Help me remember that I am secure in You when I feel shaken and insecure. Help me cling to You and also find rest in knowing that You cling to me. May I always remember that in the storm of anxiety, it is You who holds me fast.

Afflicted Saint, to Christ Draw Near

JOHN FAWCETT

Afflicted saint, to Christ draw near,
Thy Saviour's gracious promise hear;
His faithful word declares to thee,
That as thy day thy strength shall be.

Let not thy heart despond, and say,
"How shall I stand the trying day?"
He has engaged by firm decree,
That as thy day thy strength shall be.

Thy faith is weak, thy foes are strong,
And if the conflict should be long,
Thy Lord will make the tempter flee,
For as thy day thy strength shall be.

Should persecution rage and flame,
Still trust in thy Redeemer's name;
In fiery trials thou shalt see
That as thy day thy strength shall be.

AFFLICTED SAINT, TO CHRIST DRAW NEAR

What keeps you from drawing near to Christ when you are anxious? There may be several reasons why we do not draw near to Jesus in times of fear. We could be seeking to rely on our own self-sufficiency, trying to push down our anxiety, or doubting that Jesus can help. Perhaps we do not come to Jesus because we do not think He understands. We can think He does not know what we are going through, so why go to Him at all? However, Jesus does know what we are experiencing, for God the Father sent Him to the earth to suffer and die for our sins. He knows what it is like to experience suffering in many forms, including the anxiety He felt before His death. Jesus was called a man of suffering (Isaiah 53:3) who knew grief, oppression, and rejection. Jesus knows what we feel and wants us to draw near to Him so that we can receive His comfort.

2 Corinthians 1:3-5 tells us that God is a God of comfort who comforts us in all our affliction. God knows how to comfort us in our affliction perfectly because He, too, was afflicted. When we are anxious, we can feel welcome to draw near to Jesus, knowing He is not repulsed, confused, or angered by our anxiety. He understands us and covers us with His perfect comfort. When we come to Jesus, we also receive His strength. Jesus endured His suffering with incredible strength—strength that we do not possess in our own power. Jesus desires to give us His strength that we may fight against anxious thoughts and endure through moments of anxiety.

> *He understands us and covers us with His perfect comfort.*

As believers, we never suffer through our affliction alone, nor are we left without help in times of affliction. Jesus is always near to us, but we also need to draw near to Him. James 4:8 tells us, "Draw near to God, and he will draw near to you." This does not mean that God is only near to us when we seek to be close to Him, but it does mean we experience God's near presence more powerfully when we draw near to Him. To better understand this, consider a crackling fire. Standing at a far distance from the fire, you may see that the fire is there but not feel its warmth. You must draw near to the fire to experience the warmth it provides. In the same way, Jesus is always near and available to us. If we want to experience His presence more intimately, we must draw near to Him, and the best way we can draw near is to go to Him through prayer and God's Word. If you are afflicted by anxiety today, dear saint, draw near to Christ and rest in Him.

Jesus is always near and available to us.

PRAYER

Jesus, thank You that I can come to You when I am afflicted with anxiety. Thank You for welcoming me to You, for understanding my affliction, and for wanting to help me in my affliction. Ultimately, thank You for experiencing affliction so that I could receive salvation and freedom. Remind me that when I am anxious, You draw near to me, and may this reminder cause me to draw near to You. Help me rely and rest on the strength that You give me. You are my greatest comfort and help in every moment of anxiety.

Leaning on the Everlasting Arms

E. A. HOFFMAN (1887)

What a fellowship, what a joy divine,
leaning on the everlasting arms;
what a blessedness, what a peace is mine,
leaning on the everlasting arms.

CHORUS
Leaning, leaning,
safe and secure from all alarms;
leaning, leaning,
leaning on the everlasting arms.

O how sweet to walk in this pilgrim way,
leaning on the everlasting arms;
O how bright the path grows from day to day,
leaning on the everlasting arms.

What have I to dread, what have I to fear,
leaning on the everlasting arms?
I have blessed peace with my Lord so near,
leaning on the everlasting arms.

LEANING ON THE EVERLASTING ARMS

In the 1992 Olympics, runner Derek Redmond was competing in the 400-meter sprint when he suddenly snapped his hamstring. Even though he was in immense pain, he struggled forward to finish the race. Feeling someone behind him, Derek turned to see that his father had run onto the course, and wrapping his arms around Derek, his father helped carry him to the finish line. This is a picture of what God does for His children. As our Heavenly Father, God wraps His arms around us when we are anxious, allowing us to lean on Him for strength and support.

Scripture often compares the Christian life to a race. This race is not always easy, as we experience obstacles along the way and weariness as we press on to our eternal destination with Christ. Yet, we are not alone in the race. God does not stand on the sidelines, watching us struggle to move forward. Rather, He gives us the strength we need to keep going. When anxiety hits, it can be extremely difficult to keep moving forward. But when we lean on the Lord, we receive His strength that helps us fight against our anxious thoughts, empowering us to move forward.

> *He gives us the strength we need to keep going.*

Isaiah 40:28-31 tells us how God "never becomes faint or weary... He gives strength to the faint and strengthens the powerless. Youths may become faint and weary, and young men stumble and fall, but those who trust in the Lord will renew their strength; they will soar on wings like eagles; they will run and not become weary, they will walk and not faint." God gives power to the powerless because His strength is infinite. We may grow weary, but God never does. He is our source of everlasting strength.

However, we will continue fighting against our desire to rely on our own strength. Leaning on the Lord's strength is a continual act of dependency. We must surrender our self-sufficiency so that we can rest in God's sufficiency. As we lean on the Lord in our struggle with anxiety, we are also given His peace. And that perfect peace envelops us and helps ease our minds and comfort our hearts.

> We may grow weary, but God never does. He is our source of everlasting strength.

PRAYER

Lord, thank You for Your everlasting arms. Thank You that You are my constant source of strength when I am weary in the fight against anxiety. Help me lean on Your arms instead of leaning on my own strength. Help me rely on Your sufficiency alone. May I depend on You in every moment of anxiety and always turn to You for strength and peace. In Your everlasting arms, I am safe and secure.

My Hope is Built on Nothing Less

EDWARD MOTE (1834)

My hope is built on nothing less
than Jesus's blood and righteousness;
I dare not trust the sweetest frame,
but wholly lean on Jesus's name.

CHORUS
On Christ, the solid Rock, I stand:
all other ground is sinking sand;
all other ground is sinking sand.

When darkness veils His lovely face,
I rest on His unchanging grace;
in every high and stormy gale,
my anchor holds within the veil.

His oath, His covenant, His blood,
support me in the whelming flood;
when all around my soul gives way,
He then is all my hope and stay.

When He shall come with trumpet sound,
O may I then in Him be found:
dressed in His righteousness alone,
faultless to stand before the throne.

MY HOPE IS BUILT ON NOTHING LESS

Sometimes, it may feel as though we are being hit by wave after wave of anxious thoughts. Our foundation matters in these moments or seasons when anxiety fills us, for where we choose to anchor ourselves impacts our stability amid anxiety. We often try to anchor ourselves to things apart from Christ, and while relationships and things of this world can be helpful in some ways, they are not concrete foundations and cannot provide the lasting comfort we need. There is only one true foundation that can keep us grounded when waves of fear come, and that foundation is Christ.

In Isaiah 28:16, the Lord says, "Look, I have laid a stone in Zion, a tested stone, a precious cornerstone, a sure foundation; the one who believes will be unshakable." Hundreds of years before Christ came, God promised that Jesus would be a cornerstone, a strong foundation that God's people would be built upon. As believers, our lives are built upon the foundation of the gospel—the life, death, and resurrection of Christ. Without that foundation, there would be nothing to ground our faith. Christ's grace alone is what saves and sustains us.

> *Christ's grace alone is what saves us and sustains us.*

The grace of Christ gives us security in our salvation, but Christ's grace also keeps us secure in the hardships of life. Though we will indeed experience suffering in this life, Christ keeps us secure in moments of suffering by providing us with His strength. Unlike standing on sinking sand, Christ is a solid rock whose strength helps us remain immovable. Even when waves of anxiety come, they cannot shake us from our permanent foundation in Christ.

The grace of Christ also brings us hope in our anxiety. Not only is our salvation rooted in Christ but so is our hope. Because our salvation with Christ is secure, we have hope that this world will not be our home forever. The anxiety we feel is a result of living in a broken world, and in moments of fear, if we do not place our hope in Christ, we can believe the lie that this suffering will be a reality forever. As believers, our hope is to be placed in the truth that one day Christ will return and usher in a world free from sin. If we hope in anything else when we feel anxious, we will surely be disappointed, yet when we hope in Jesus, we will experience joy, even amid fear.

Because Christ is our solid rock, we can lean on Him in times of fear. We can cling to Him, knowing that Jesus anchors us in the storms of anxiety. And even when anxiety leaves us shaken, we can be reminded that in Christ, we are secure. Jesus remains a strong foundation, even as the world around us gives way.

> *Because Christ is our solid rock, we can lean on Him in times of fear.*

PRAYER

Jesus, thank You for being my solid rock, anchor, and hope. Thank You that when anxiety seeks to sway me, I can remain steadfast in You. Help me cling to You tightly in moments of fear. Forgive me for the times that I go to the things of this world for a foundation, when my one true foundation is You. Help me place my hope in You when I am afraid, trusting in You alone. May I lean on You and depend on You when I feel overwhelmed by anxiety. Only You can keep me steady when waves of anxiety come.

Blessed Assurance

FANNY CROSBY (1873)

Blessed assurance, Jesus is mine!
Oh, what a foretaste of glory divine!
Heir of salvation, purchase of God,
born of His Spirit, washed in His blood.

CHORUS
This is my story, this is my song,
praising my Savior all the day long.
This is my story, this is my song,
praising my Savior all the day long.

Perfect communion, perfect delight,
visions of rapture now burst on my sight.
Angels descending bring from above
echoes of mercy, whispers of love.

Perfect submission, all is at rest.
I in my Savior am happy and bless'd,
watching and waiting, looking above,
filled with His goodness, lost in His love.

BLESSED ASSURANCE

A lie that may often enter the mind of anxious believers is that real Christians do not struggle with anxiety. This lie can not only make us feel ashamed over our struggles with anxiety but make us doubt if we are genuine believers. This lie is a lie from the enemy, seeking to turn us away from the Lord. But, instead of fixating on the enemy's lies, we need to rest in the truth of our assurance in Christ. Regardless of our struggle with anxiety, we belong to Jesus and are forever loved by Him.

Our assurance as believers is rooted in Christ's grace. Jesus is the One who saved us, who transformed our hearts by His grace. We have been washed with His blood, and the punishment for our sin has been removed. Christ's grace has brought us into a precious union with God and ensures us an eternity with Him. His grace sustains us no matter what we do or experience in this life. Even in our struggle with anxiety, Christ's grace remains.

> *Our assurance as believers is rooted in Christ's grace.*

When the enemy seeks to make us ashamed of our suffering, we must remember what God's Word says. Throughout Scripture, we see that suffering is a reality for all believers due to the brokenness of a sinful world. While suffering is inevitable, God uses suffering in our lives uniquely. As followers of Christ, we reflect Jesus, who suffered for our sake, when we experience suffering. We reflect His perseverance and endurance as we press forward, trusting God through every trial and trouble. And we not only reflect Christ, but we become like Christ as we experience suffering. God uses our suffering to sanctify us, shape us, and refine us into the image of Christ. While God does not enjoy watching His children suffer, He allows us to experience suffering so that we can depend on Him, grow in our faith, and become more like Jesus.

Both the reality of our suffering and the work of God through our suffering brings hope for believers. Instead of feeling ashamed of our anxiety, we can be comforted as we remember that God is working through our anxiety. We can also be comforted as we dwell on God's love for us. Because of our salvation, we are loved by God no matter what. No matter our struggle with suffering or sin, God always loves us and gives us His grace. When anxiety comes, we can fight the enemy's lies with the truth that nothing can separate us from the love of God (Romans 8:39).

There is blessed assurance for every believer who is anxiety-laden. Because of our salvation in Christ, there is no shame for the believer—only joy, hope, and peace. May we rest in the assurance that Christ's grace gives us when the enemy seeks to fill us with doubt and shame. We are Christ's, and He is ours, forever.

> *We are Christ's, and He is ours, forever.*

PRAYER

Jesus, thank You that there is blessed assurance for me. Thank You that I always remain in You, even though I struggle with anxiety. When the enemy seeks to make me feel doubt and shame, remind me of who I am to You. Remind me that I belong to You and that You always give me your grace and mercy. Help me trust You, God, when I feel anxious, knowing that You are using even this suffering to shape me into the image of Your Son. Please give me the strength to endure as I look ahead to the eternity that is to come.

His Eye is On the Sparrow

CIVILLA D. MARTIN (1905)

Why should I feel discouraged,
Why should the shadows come,
Why should my heart be lonely,
And long for heav'n and home;
When Jesus is my portion?
My constant Friend is He;
His eye is on the sparrow,
And I know He watches me;
His eye is on the sparrow,
And I know He watches me.

CHORUS
I sing because I'm happy,
I sing because I'm free;
For His eye is on the sparrow,
And I know He watches me.

"Let not your heart be troubled,"
His tender word I hear,
And resting on His goodness,
I lose my doubts and fears;
Though by the path He leadeth,
But one step I may see;
His eye is on the sparrow,
And I know He watches me;
His eye is on the sparrow,
And I know He watches me.

Whenever I am tempted,
Whenever clouds arise;
When songs give place to sighing,
When hope within me dies,
I draw the closer to Him,
From care He sets me free;
His eye is on the sparrow,
And I know He watches me;
His eye is on the sparrow,
And I know He watches me.

HIS EYE IS ON THE SPARROW

Before Jesus ascended into heaven, He told His disciples, "Peace I leave with you. My peace I give to you. I do not give to you as the world gives. Don't let your heart be troubled or fearful" (John 14:27). Jesus's instruction to not let our hearts be afraid is not a harsh rebuke but a tender word. Jesus desires our hearts to be at peace instead of fearful, and He has given us His perfect peace to help calm our worried hearts.

But even still, it can be hard to feel at peace when circumstances feel out of control. When life is hectic and troubles arise, we can struggle to trust in Jesus and experience His peace. One of the ways we can have peace in moments of fear is to remember God's care for us. In Matthew 6:25-34, Jesus calls us to look at the birds and see how God provides for their needs. He reminds us that if God takes care of the birds, He will surely take care of His children. Just like God keeps His eye on the birds, God always watches over us. God is a heavenly Father who watches over His children.

> *God is a heavenly Father who watches over His children.*

God's watchful eye declares how there is nothing in our lives that God misses or overlooks. And God not only sovereignly watches over everything but sovereignly works through everything. God's sovereignty reveals that God is not a passive bystander but an active participant in our lives. He not only sees our fears, but He works through what makes us afraid. Though our circumstances may be trying, we can find comfort in knowing that nothing surprises God, and nothing is beyond His control. We can have peace in moments of fear as we trust and rest in God's sovereignty.

God's sovereignty also encourages us to move forward in times of fear. We do not have to remain stuck in anxiety, afraid to step into the plans God has for us. We can walk where the Lord leads, even if it is one shaky step at a time. Because God is always watching over us and guiding us, we can choose to trust Him as we step out in faith, even if we do not understand what He is doing. We remember that all God has planned for us is for His glory and our good. By His grace, God leads us through our lives, promising to watch over us and provide for us, every step of the way.

When anxieties arise, look to the birds of the sky, and remember that God is watching over you. Let their song remind you that you can sing in times of fear because of God's sovereign control over all things. He will work through those things that make you afraid—no matter how difficult the circumstance. So rest in His sovereignty, and sink into His perfect peace.

PRAYER

Dear Lord, thank You for always watching over me. Thank You that I never leave Your sight and that You desire to guide me and take care of me. When I feel afraid, help me remember that You are here with me. Help me remember that You are working through whatever is making me afraid. Help me trust in Your sovereignty when life feels out of control. Because You work all things for my good and Your glory, I can trust You. There is nothing beyond Your control, so may I rest in Your perfect sovereignty. Your eye is on the sparrow, and therefore it will always be on me.

Wonderful Peace

W. D. CORNELL

Far away in the depths of my spirit tonight
Rolls a melody sweeter than psalm;
In celestial-like strains it unceasingly falls
O'er my soul like an infinite calm.

CHORUS
Peace! Peace! wonderful peace,
Coming down from the Father above;
Sweep over my spirit forever, I pray,
In fathomless billows of love.

What a treasure I have in this wonderful peace,
Buried deep in the heart of my soul;
So secure that no power can mine it away,
While the years of eternity roll.

I am resting tonight in this wonderful peace,
Resting sweetly in Jesus's control;
For I'm kept from all danger by night and by day,
And His glory is flooding my soul.

And methinks when I rise to that City of peace,
Where the Author of peace I shall see,
That one strain of the song which the ransomed will sing,
In that heavenly kingdom shall be.

Ah! soul, are you here without comfort or rest,
Marching down the rough pathway of time?
Make Jesus your friend ere the shadows grow dark;
Oh, accept this sweet peace so sublime.

WONDERFUL PEACE

When we are anxious, all we want is peace. We want to feel calm instead of chaotic, settled instead of shaken. As believers, it can be hard to remember that peace is always available to us. Because we cannot see God, it can be easier to look for peace in tangible ways. God may be invisible to us, but that does not mean we cannot experience His peace. God's presence is always with us through the Spirit, which means God's peace is always with us.

As followers of Christ, we have been given peace with God through Christ's death and resurrection. Christ's grace given to us and our faith in Him restores our once-broken relationship with God, ensuring a relationship of complete peace between God and us. And because God is a God of peace, we are in a relationship with the only One who can give us true and lasting peace. Although we cannot see God, we can go to God's Word and see evidence of His love for us and the peace that He provides. We can go to Him in prayer and experience His peaceful presence as we draw near to Him. And the best part of God's peace is that it can never be taken from us. Our relationship with the Lord is one that is permanent. Because our relationship with God is secure, so too is the peace we have with Christ.

God's peace is always with us.

One of the best ways we can rest in God's peace is to remind ourselves of the peace that is to come. One day, we will be united with our Savior, and we will see the author of peace face to face. We will live in a world free from darkness and sin, and we will dwell within a city of peace with God forever. We struggle now, but we remember that one day all we will know is the fullness of His peace. And even in the here and now, we have a glimpse of that peace through the presence and power of the Holy Spirit.

We do not have to allow our anxiety to keep us from experiencing God's peace. When fears rain heavily upon us, we can turn to the Lord and cling to Him. We can turn to His Word and allow the truths of Scripture to wash over us. And when the day is done, we can rest in God's peace. As we lay our heads on our pillows, we can rest in knowing that we are kept in God's hands. We can rest in knowing that Christ is in control of our circumstances. We can rest in knowing that God's peace surrounds us and flows within us. There is wonderful peace available to every believer in Christ, so let us, without hesitation, turn to Jesus and rest in His perfect peace.

Our relationship with the Lord is one that is permanent.

PRAYER

Lord, thank You for Your wonderful peace. Thank You that Your peace is always available to me in every moment of fear. In times of fear, help me go to You for peace. Help me rest in You and You alone. May I press through my anxiety, knowing that one day all I will know is Your wonderful peace. But in the here and now, may I rest in the peace that is given to me through Christ and by Your Spirit.

'Tis So Sweet to Trust in Jesus

LOUISA M. R. STEAD (1882)

'Tis so sweet to trust in Jesus,
just to take Him at His Word;
just to rest upon His promise,
Just to know, "Thus saith the Lord."

CHORUS
Jesus, Jesus, how I trust Him!
How I've proved Him o'er and o'er!
Jesus, Jesus, precious Jesus!
O for grace to trust Him more!

O how sweet to trust in Jesus,
just to trust His cleansing blood;
and in simple faith to plunge me
neath the healing, cleansing flood!

Yes, 'tis sweet to trust in Jesus,
just from sin and self to cease;
just from Jesus simply taking
life and rest, and joy and peace.

I'm so glad I learned to trust Thee,
Precious Jesus, Savior, Friend;
And I know that Thou art with me,
Wilt be with me to the end.

'TIS SO SWEET TO TRUST IN JESUS

Do you have a friend you can trust with anything? Someone who will always be faithful to help you, listen to you, and love you? A friend who has demonstrated their faithfulness and dependability to you time and time again is a friend you know you can count on and trust. However, even the most reliable friend will fail you at some point. But, unlike a friend who can waver in their trustworthiness, Jesus is trustworthy always.

Because Jesus is God, He never changes, lies, or fails to come through. So why then do we struggle to trust Him? We can read what Scripture says about who Jesus is and what He has done for us and struggle to believe those verses are always true. Maybe we trust in Jesus when things are going well, but when trials come and anxiety rises, our trust can falter.

Jesus is trustworthy always.

If we find ourselves struggling to trust Jesus in moments of anxiety, all we must do is go to God's Word. Because Scripture is the Word of God, everything Scripture says about Jesus is trustworthy and true. We can trust that when Jesus said, "It is finished" on the cross (John 19:30), He truly accomplished our salvation. We can trust that when Jesus said, "I will be with you always" (Matthew 28:20), He meant it. We can trust that when He said, "Come to me . . . and and I will give you rest" (Matthew 11:28), His words were true. Jesus is the same yesterday, today, and forever. Because He is unchanging, His character and promises never change.

Knowing somebody's character either encourages or discourages our trust in them. Jesus's character makes it sweet to trust Him.

When Jesus calls us to come to Him for rest, He declares that He is lowly and humble in heart (Matthew 11:29). Jesus is not a malicious, fickle, or unjust God. His character is trustworthy because Jesus is a gentle, gracious, and good God. Jesus beckons us to Him with loving words and a warm embrace, encouraging us to trust Him with whatever is making us afraid.

Jesus is our reliable, dependable, and faithful friend. What joy to trust in Jesus, for we will never have to wonder if Jesus will let us down. Jesus will always be faithful to us and will always give us what we need. When we are anxious, we can always count on Jesus to help us. We can always count on Him to give us His peace and strength. And we can always count on Jesus never to leave us or forsake us. A friend may struggle to remain dependable in troubling seasons, but Jesus will always remain dependable. He will not abandon us when situations in our lives become weighty and when our anxiety grows heavy. 'Tis so sweet to trust in Jesus because He is our precious Savior and faithful friend.

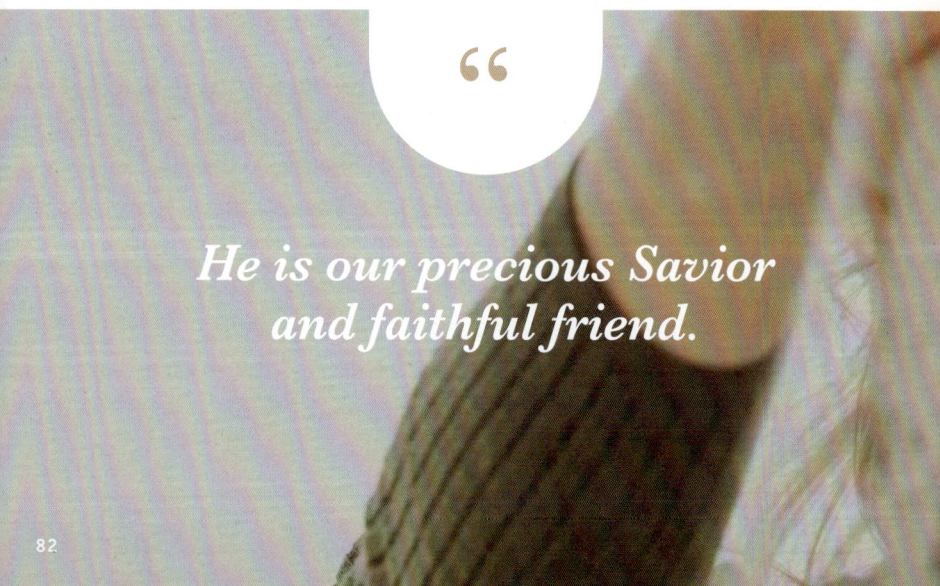

> *He is our precious Savior and faithful friend.*

PRAYER

Jesus, thank You for being trustworthy. Thank You that You are a good, gracious, and kind God who never changes and never lies. When I am anxious, help me trust You. Help me remember who You are and what You have done for me through Your death and resurrection. Help me remember what You promise in God's Word. May I cling to You tightly in moments of fear, fully trusting that You will help me through whatever it is that makes me afraid.

Thank you for studying God's Word with us!

CONNECT WITH US
@THEDAILYGRACECO
@DAILYGRACEPODCAST

CONTACT US
INFO@THEDAILYGRACECO.COM

SHARE
#THEDAILYGRACECO

VISIT US ONLINE
WWW.THEDAILYGRACECO.COM

MORE DAILY GRACE
THE DAILY GRACE APP
DAILY GRACE PODCAST